D0564519

CAPPUCCINO/ESPRESSO
THE BOOK OF BEVERAGES

Christie Katona
Thomas Katona

BRISTOL PUBLISHING ENTERPRISES
San Leandro, California

A Nitty Gritty® Cookbook

©1993 Bristol Publishing Enterprises, Inc.
P.O. Box 1737, San Leandro, California 94577.
World rights reserved. No part of this publication
may be reproduced by any mechanical, photo-
graphic, or electronic process, or in the form of
a phonographic recording, nor may it be stored
in a retrieval system, transmitted, or otherwise
copied for public or private use without prior
written permission from the publisher.

Printed in the United States of America.

ISBN 1-55867-099-8

Cover design: Frank Paredes
Cover photography: John Benson
Food stylist: Suzanne Carreiro
Illustrator: James Balkovek

CONTENTS

ESPRESSO-BASED DRINKS: THE BASICS

In 1992 we wrote *The Coffee Book*, also published by Bristol Publishing. That book has a collection of delicious food recipes that either use coffee or go well with coffee. While the *The Coffee Book* includes several coffee drinks, our publisher could see a need for a book dedicated to coffee drinks. When we started to do the research for this book, we discovered how true that was.

We found that published information on coffee drinks was scarce to the point of being almost nonexistent. As a result, we turned to those people who would be most knowledgeable about espresso and espresso drinks, the espresso stand owners and operators, and the suppliers who cater to them. The more interesting drink combinations inside this book are the result of the suggestions and recipes generously shared by those entrepreneurs, operators and business people. We also have to confess to some enthusiastic experimenting on our part.

We have what we think is a great collection of recipes that include espressos, cappuccinos, lattes, Italian sodas, cold drinks for hot summer days, and spirited drinks for cold winter nights. We are glad we can bring these together in one book so you can enjoy them too.

A LITTLE HISTORY

By most accounts, the discovery of coffee took place around 600 A.D. It is widely believed that Ethiopian tribesmen discovered the coffee plant growing in the wild while tending their herds. The tribesmen mixed the ground berries with animal fat and rolled the resulting mixture into balls for eating during their journeys. For the next 400 years the berries were used primarily for food (although some resourceful person discovered the berries could be fermented into wine). The use and cultivation of the beans eventually migrated to Arabia where somewhere between 10th and 15th centuries (the scholars are still arguing about when), the Arabs learned to steep the beans in water to make a delicious brew they called *qahwa* which translates to something like "that which makes one able to do without something" (without sleep?). The brew, considered by some to be a potent medicine, was known for its restorative powers as well as being a delicious beverage. By the end of the 15th century Arabian coffee houses were popular meeting places and coffee was an established part of Arabian life.

As early as the 13th century, Arabia was shipping coffee from Arabian ports including Mocha, which is the source of the name for this famous coffee bean. The enterprising Arabian merchants who grew and sold the beans shrewdly prevented any viable seeds and coffee plants from being exported to protect their monopoly on the product. For several hundred years they were successful at keeping the source of the beans to themselves and enjoyed a brisk trade and high profits.

However, as we all know, it is hard to keep a good thing to yourself forever. In the 17th century it is reputed that a Moslem pilgrim was successful at smuggling a plant and/or seeds home to his native India. From this humble start, the first coffee plantation in India was started at Karnatak and quickly spread to dozens of countries within a very short span of time. Dutch traders purchased some of the trees from the Karnatak plantation and began cultivating them in Java, which is the source of the Mocha Java blend.

A young French naval officer, Captain Gabriel Mathieu de Clieu, is credited with being responsible for bringing the plant to the Caribbean via Martinique where it spread throughout the West Indies and eventually to Central and South America. The single plant he brought to Martinique appears to be the progenitor of most of the billions of coffee plants which are now the major source of the world's coffee. The plant acquired (stolen) by De Clieu was a descendent of a coffee plant given as a gift to Louis XIV. The king's coffee plants were cultivated in a hothouse at Louie XIV's Jardin des Plantes and were kept under close guard. De Clieu was able to obtain one of the plants through a romantic liaison with a lady of the court who had access to the hothouse; the rest is history.

Romance also played a part in the spread of coffee production to Brazil. There is evidence that Brazil clandestinely acquired the plant through Dutch Guianna, where a Brazilian Army Lieutenant smuggled the plant back to Brazil with the aid of the wife of the local governor, who was enamored with the Lieutenant.

Coffee spread from Arabia first to Turkey and eventually to Europe. It appears that Venetian traders were responsible for introducing coffee to European markets. The first coffee house in England opened in 1637 and within three decades had spread throughout the country. English coffee houses became a center for social, intellectual, commercial, and political discussions. These coffee houses became known as "penny universities," because by paying a penny admission price, you could hear intellectual discussions as well as the latest gossip and news while enjoying your cup of coffee.

In the American colonies, the Dutch had introduced English-style coffee houses, but up to the American revolution and the Boston Tea Party, tea was the preferred American beverage. Starting with the boycott of English tea, the beverage of choice in America became coffee and to date has remained the preferred beverage for most Americans.

ESPRESSO

All the coffee recipes in this book are based on espresso as the main ingredient, so you will want to be able to make a good espresso as the starting point.

In the past, most people associated the term *espresso* with a concentrated and bitter brew. However, there has been a new awareness of espresso and high quality coffees in general created within the last five years due to articles in magazines, newspapers, and to promotions by the coffee industry. As a result, the general public has become more sophisticated and discerning in their taste, and the old reputation for espresso has been replaced by an enthusiam for espresso-based drinks as evidenced by the long lines at the espresso stands.

The term *espresso* is Italian for *fast* and primarily describes the method of preparation. The espresso method uses pressure rather than gravity to rapidly extract the essence of the coffee in a concentrated form. *Espresso* is also used to describe the blend of beans and the degree of roast for the beans used to prepare espresso. Espresso roast is one of the darkest roasts and is characterized by a slightly burnt flavor.

Almost all coffee specialty shops now have commercial espresso machines and serve both pure espresso and derivative espresso drinks to a growing number of enthusiasts. In the Seattle area, espresso has become something of a phenomenon.

In addition to the specialty shops, curbside espresso carts and drive-through espresso windows have sprung up throughout the greater metropolitan area and it seems that every shopping mall and supermarket has its own espresso station.

Automated espresso machines are also becoming common in cafeterias and at convenience stores in our area of the country. The first do-it-yourself commercial machines that hit the market did not do a very good job. They generally overextracted the coffee and produced a very bitter espresso. However, progress has been made and the most recent versions of these machines are very sophisticated and do a much better job than their predecessors. The best of these machines have digital readouts, offer choices in size, strength, type of drink, and even the addition of flavors. Although they cannot offer the range of choices offered by an espresso cart, we have been hard-pressed to taste a difference between hand-brewed and computer-brewed with some of the better machines.

At the beginning of the espresso rage, demand was greater than the supply and the espresso shop/cart owner had a very lucrative business with more customers than he could handle. Not counting his investment, he was generally selling the drinks at 8-10 times his material costs for coffee, milk, flavorings, and cups and napkins. Now, with so many espresso competitors, the prices have started to drop and operators are offering incentives to get customers to buy from their store or cart versus the competitor across the street. Our local grocery store provides a coupon for a free latte with the purchase of $50 or more of groceries. Many of the drive-through latte stands now offer punch cards which give you a free drink after you accumulate a certain number of punches. The best deal we have found so far is buy four and get the fifth for free with no limitation on the size. Isn't competition wonderful!?

If you decide to prepare your own espresso at home, there are many espresso machines available in the specialty stores intended for home use. These range from less expensive "Moka" pots which are heated on your burner to very sophisticated espresso machines. Prices for the automatic machines run from just under $100 to about $700 depending on the features and quality desired. Achilles Gaggia is credited with making the first modern espresso machine at the end of World War II. Gaggia's machine replaced steam pressure with a mechanical piston which provided much better control over the pressure.

All of the espresso machines work by forcing hot, pressurized water through finely ground espresso coffee that is tamped into a filter basket to make individual cups of espresso. Since pressure is used to extract the coffee essence, the variables of grind, quantity, tamp and rate of pour have a greater influence on the final taste than they do in the regular gravity feed drip coffee pots used for most home-brewed coffee.

You will have to experiment with the four variables since different brand machines have different operating pressures. Generally, the higher the operating pressure, the finer the grind of coffee you will use. Home machines generally operate in the area of

130 pounds per square inch (psi). The ideal water temperature is 193° to 197 °F, which may or may not be adjustable on your machine.

The more sophisticated models from each manufacturer also provide a cappuccino nozzle that uses the steam generated by the machine to steam and froth milk for cappuccinos, lattes and steamers. Many of the recipes in this book make use of a cappuccino nozzle and we recommend you purchase an espresso machine which comes with this attachment.

Regardless of the equipment you choose to use, there are a few essentials to making good espresso at home:

1. Start with good quality, freshly roasted espresso beans.
2. Use clean equipment.
3. Use fresh water.
4. Use the correct grind and wait until just before making your espresso to grind the beans.
5. Use the right amount of coffee.
6. Use the right water temperature (automatic on the better machines).
7. Serve immediately after pouring.

The importance of good quality coffee beans is paramount. If you start with inferior beans, you can't expect to brew a great cup of espresso. Clean equipment is important as well. Remember that coffee contains oils and other substances that get deposited on your equipment which can taint the flavor of the next cup if not removed.

If you're lucky to have a clean, fresh tasting water supply in your city, then cool running tap water will make a great cup of espresso. If your water has enough minerals or other substances to alter the taste, then consider a water filter or bottled spring water. If using tap water, let the cold water run for a time to aerate the water. Remember that your end product is still mostly water.

Beyond using good quality beans, fresh water and clean equipment, the secret to making good espresso is to avoid either under- or over-extracting the coffee essence. If the grind is too fine or the tamping too tight, the flow will be restricted, resulting in an over-extracted and bitter espresso. If the grind is too course or if the grinds are not tamped tightly enough, the water will flow too quickly, resulting in a thin and insipid espresso.

The right amount of espresso coffee is determined by the capacity of your machine. Generally, you will fill your filter insert almost completely, leaving just a little room for expansion of the grounds. Most home machines use about $1\frac{1}{2}$ tablespoons per cup. The rate of pour is best determined by experiment; however, as a guideline your machine should produce about 1 to $1\frac{1}{4}$ ounces of espresso in about 25 seconds for a single shot machine.

If your cup of espresso has a creamy golden froth on top after the pour, you have done a good job. The dense foam topping is called the *crema* and is a sign that you have brewed a full-bodied and flavorful espresso.

ESPRESSO BAR BASICS

You will find that there is an enormous variety of espresso-based drinks as well as flavored steamed milk drinks available at the espresso bars. Below is a list of the basics you should find at any modern espresso stand:

Breve	A latte made with steamed half and half
Café Americano	Filtered hot water added to a shot of espresso (full-flavored and satisfying yet mild as brewed coffee)
Café Latte	A shot of espresso added to steamed and foamed milk. Many flavors are available for the nonpurist. (Christie's favorite is almond).
Café Mocha	Espresso mixed with steamed milk and chocolate syrup and usually topped with whipped cream sprinkled with cocoa powder

Cappuccino	Its name is derived from the foamy cap on the drink which resembles the long, pointed cowl, or cappuccino, worn by Capuchin friars. A "wet" cappuccino is made by using approximately $1/3$ espresso, $1/3$ hot steamed milk, and $1/3$ foamed milk. A "dry" cappuccino is a shot of espresso with the remainder of the cup filled with foam.
Espresso Con Panna	An espresso topped with a dollop of whipped cream.
Espresso Doppio	Similar to ristretto but with two shots of espresso and served in a small cup
Espresso Macchiato	An espresso "marked" with a dollop of milk foam (Note: Macchiato is pronounced MOCK-E-AH-TOE)
Espresso Ristretto	A short pour (less than 1 ounce) which is accomplished by turning of the pump a few seconds earlier than normal.
Espresso Romano	An espresso served with a lemon wedge or the zest of a lemon
Latte Macchiato	A cup of steamed milk "marked" with a spot of espresso. The steamed milk is added first, then topped with foam, and the espresso is added last by pouring it through the foam which leaves the "mark."

Steamer	Steamed milk with a flavored syrup. Almond, vanilla, and hazelnut are popular. In addition, there are flavors available that range from the interesting to the bizarre.

TIPS FOR STEAMING MILK

For those who purchase espresso machines with a steam nozzle, the following steps should help you make better lattes, steamers and cappuccinos.

1. If you want a lot of foam, use low fat milks (nonfat, 1%, and 2%); use whole milk for richer drinks (but with less foam).
2. Use a clean and cold stainless steel pitcher. Using a steel pitcher will allow you to feel the milk's temperature as you heat the milk.
3. Fill the pitcher about one-third its capacity with fresh cold milk.
4. Open the steam valve briefly to bleed the steam nozzle of condensed water before steaming.
5. Insert the nozzle into the milk and open the steam valve fully.
6. Lower the pitcher until the nozzle is just below the surface of the milk and keep it there until sufficient foam is built for your purposes. For cappuccinos, let the foam rise to the top of the pitcher.

7. After the foam has been built, lower the nozzle into the milk to continue the heating process. The ideal temperature is about 150° F which is about the point where the pitcher becomes too hot to hold for more than a second. If you want to be sure, use a thermometer.

8. Turn off the steam and remove the pitcher from the nozzle. Let the pitcher of steamed milk settle for a few minutes, which gives you time to prepare your espresso and let the foam thicken a bit.

9. For cappuccino-style drinks, use a spoon to hold back the foam while pouring the steamed milk over the espresso, and then spoon the thick foam over the steamed milk and espresso to provide the foam cap from which cappuccino derives its name. The process is similar for lattes, steamers, breves, etc., except less foam is used.

SIZES AND STRENGTHS

Whether you are buying from an espresso cart or creating your own drinks at home, following is a list of the basic terms used to describe the size and strengths of the drinks found at espresso stands.

Sizes

Short/Regular: 8-ounce cup
Tall/Medium: 12-ounce cup

Grande: 16-ounce cup

Strengths

Single: 1 shot of espresso
Double: 2 shots of espresso

Triple: 3 shots of espresso
Quad: 4 shots of espresso

FLAVORED SYRUPS

There are many flavored syrups on the market today. Some of the most popular brands are Torani, DaVinci and Pasanos. The syrups originated in Italy where they were used to flavor Italian sodas. It all started when the Torani Company brought its products to the United States in 1925. Now there are dozens of flavors on the market to use in coffee drinks, Italian-style sodas and other recipes. The syrups do not contain caffeine, are nonalcoholic and contain approximately 60 to 80 calories per ounce.

From the list we've included, you can create almost endless combinations to suit your personal taste. We find most of the fruit-flavored syrups are best in Italian sodas or iced drinks and the nut, spice and richer flavors are more suited to lattes, cappuccinos and mochas. Somehow the addition of chocolate to coffee rounds out the flavors and makes it more compatible with syrups such as orange, raspberry, strawberry, banana, coconut and mint.

almond	coconut	mandarindo
amaretto	coffee	mango
anisette	cranberry	maple nut
apple	creamy orange	Mediterranean grape
banana	crème de cacao	orange
bing cherry	crème de cassis	orgeat
blackberry	crème de menthe	passion fruit
blueberry	French vanilla	peach
boysenberry	ginger	peppermint
butterscotch	grand orange	pineapple
caramel	grape	raspberry
cherry	hazelnut	root beer
chocolate	Irish cream	spicy cinnamon
chocolate fudge	Kahlua coffee	strawberry
chocolate malt	kiwi	Swedish rum
chocolate mint	lemon	tamarindo
chocolate peanut butter	licorice	vanilla
cinnamon	lime	watermelon
citrus lemon	macadamia nut	

GARNISHES

The appearance of all espresso drinks can be enhanced by using just the right cup, glass or mug. Adding an appropriate garnish also gives the finished product eye appeal as well as additional flavor. Some of the manufacturers make interesting toppings, such as raspberry powder or granulated brown sugar. Rolled wafers, dainty cookies and miniature candy bars can also enhance the presentation of your special espresso drinks. Wholesale purveyors carry these items right next to the flavored syrups. Finely chopped nuts can be prepared in advance and frozen. Toasting them gives them extra flavor as well as crunch. Just a sprinkling of cocoa powder, cinnamon or nutmeg can add that special touch. Toasted coconut is easy to prepare and store. Whipped cream is always enjoyed by everyone. Adding a flavored syrup or liqueur makes it all the more special. So experiment!

Suggested Garnishes

white or dark shaved chocolate
white or dark chocolate curls
dark chocolate or multi colored sprinkles
sugar crystals - single colors and rainbow
finely chopped nuts
rolled wafers

whipped cream
flavored whipped cream
mint leaves
sliced berries, such as strawberries
whole fruits - cherries, raspberries,
 blueberries

sliced fruits - kiwi, star fruit, peaches
citrus slices - orange, lemon, lime
pineapple spears or wedges
candied citrus peel or ginger
cinnamon
cinnamon sticks
grated nutmeg
peppermint sticks

vanilla sugar
granulated brown sugar
cinnamon and brown sugar topping
chocolate and brown sugar topping
nutmeg and brown sugar topping
vanilla powder
raspberry powder
mini marshmallows

GALLIANO WHIPPED CREAM   Servings: 6-8

This is great on drinks using a licorce-type flavoring, such as sambucca or anisette.

1 cup heavy cream   1 tbs. Galliano liqueur
2 tbs. powdered sugar

In a chilled bowl, whip cream until beginning to thicken. Add sugar and liqueur. Continue beating until soft peaks form. Store covered in the refrigerator if not using immediately.

FLAVORED WHIPPED CREAM
Servings: 6-8

Any of the syrups can be used to flavor whipped cream.

½ pint heavy cream   2 tbs. flavored syrup

In a chilled bowl, whip cream until beginning to thicken. Add syrup. Continue beating until soft peaks. Store covered in the refrigerator if not using immediately.

ORANGE WHIPPED CREAM
Servings: 6-8

This makes a delightful topping for espresso drinks. Kahlua, amaretto, Frangelico or brandy can be used instead of the Grand Marnier.

1 cup heavy cream   1 tbs. Grand Marnier liqueur
2 tbs. powdered sugar

In a chilled bowl, whip cream until beginning to thicken. Add sugar and liqueur. Store covered in the refrigerator if not using immediately.

CHOCOLATE WHIPPED CREAM

Servings: 6-8

The crowning touch for so many espresso drinks. If you're not using the whipped cream immediately there is a stabilizing product on the market called **Whip It.** *Look for it at specialty gourmet stores. A small envelope will help whipped cream hold for hours.*

1 cup heavy cream   2 tbs. cocoa powder
2 tbs. powdered sugar

In a chilled bowl, whip cream until beginning to thicken. Add sugar and cocoa. Continue whipping until soft peaks form. Store covered in the refrigerator if not using immediately.

VARIATION

• Add 1 tbs. Kahlua liqueur to the whipped cream.

LATTES

CREAM DE LA CREAM

Servings: 1

This latte is truly a cut above the ordinary.

1 oz. crème de cacao syrup
1 oz. Irish cream syrup
1 shot espresso
steamed milk
whipped cream
vanilla powder for garnish

In an 8-ounce cup, combine syrups and espresso. Fill cup with steamed milk, top with whipped cream and garnish with vanilla powder.

APPLE PIE LATTE

Servings: 1

Old-fashioned goodness in a cup.

> 1 oz. apple syrup
> dash of cinnamon syrup
> 1 shot espresso
> steamed milk
> cinnamon for garnish

Combine syrups and expresso in an 8-ounce cup. Fill with steamed milk, top with foam and sprinkle with cinnamon.

BAKLAVA LATTE

All the flavors of that rich Middle Eastern dessert in a latte!

1 oz. praline syrup
½ oz. hazelnut syrup
½ oz. maple walnut syrup
dash of lemon syrup
2 tsp. honey
1 shot espresso
steamed milk
cinnamon for garnish
cinnamon stick for garnish

Combine syrups, honey and espresso in a 10-ounce cup. Fill with steamed milk, top with foam, sprinkle generously with cinnamon and garnish with a cinnamon stick.

CANDY BAR LATTES

With all the delicious flavors of syrups available, you can create a candy bar in a cup. Due to the fact that the names are registered trademarks, you'll have to guess which ones the following five drinks most resemble.

CHOCOLATE BUTTERSCOTCH LATTE   Servings: 1

One shop in Seattle features beautiful enameled earrings with various espresso designs on them. Seattle takes its coffee seriously!

½ oz. butterscotch ice cream topping   1 shot espresso
½ oz. chocolate syrup   steamed milk

In an 8-ounce cup, combine ice cream topping, syrup and espresso. Fill cup with steamed milk.

CARAMEL NUT LATTE

Servings: 1

If you wish to top this drink, use whipped cream and finely chopped peanuts.

1/2 oz. caramel ice cream topping
3/4 oz. chocolate ice cream topping
1/2 oz. hazelnut syrup
1 shot espresso
steamed milk
whipped cream, optional
finely chopped peanuts, optional

In an 8-ounce cup, combine toppings, syrup and espresso. Fill cup with steamed milk and top with foam. Add whipped cream and peanuts for garnish if desired.

COCONUT ALMOND DELIGHT

Servings: 1

The composer Bach liked coffee so much he named a cantata "The Coffee Cantata."

1 oz. almond syrup
½ oz. coconut syrup
1 oz. chocolate topping
1 shot espresso
steamed milk

In an 8-ounce cup, combine syrups, chocolate topping and espresso. Fill cup with steamed milk and top with foam.

CHERRY COCONUT MOCHA

Servings: 1

History says that Napoleon drank seven pots of coffee a day.

> 1 oz. chocolate topping
> ½ oz. cherry syrup
> ½ oz. coconut syrup
> 1 shot espresso
> steamed milk

In an 8-ounce cup, combine topping, syrups and espresso. Fill cup with steamed milk and top with foam.

VARIATIONS

- Use vanilla syrup instead of coconut.
- Use almond syrup instead of coconut.

COCONUT DELIGHT

Servings: 1

You can use canned cream of coconut or coconut syrup to make this drink.

1 oz. chocolate syrup
½ oz. coconut syrup
1 shot espresso

steamed milk
toasted coconut for garnish, optional

In an 8-ounce cup, combine syrups and espresso. Fill cup with steamed milk and top with foam. Garnish with toasted coconut if desired.

VARIATIONS

- Use chocolate topping instead of syrup.
- Use chocolate fudge syrup instead of syrup.
- Add ½ oz. Kahlua syrup.

FUDGE BROWNIE LATTE

Servings: 1

If your latte has an "off" green or bitter flavor, check to make sure your beans aren't old or you haven't over-extracted the grind.

1 oz. chocolate fudge syrup
½ oz. vanilla syrup
½ oz. maple nut syrup

1 shot espresso
steamed milk
cocoa powder for garnish

In an 8-ounce cup, combine syrups and espresso. Fill cup with steamed milk, top with foam and sprinkle with cocoa powder.

VARIATIONS

- Use macadamia nut syrup instead of maple nut.
- Use hazelnut syrup instead of maple nut.

ALMOND BUTTERSCOTCH LATTE
Servings: 1

When Marilyn Monroe married Arthur Miller in 1956, she used coffee to dye her white veil to match her beige dress.

½ oz. butterscotch ice cream topping
½ oz. chocolate topping
½ oz. almond syrup
1 shot espresso
steamed milk

In an 8-ounce cup, combine toppings, syrup and espresso. Fill cup with steamed milk.

HONEY NUT LATTE

Honey makes a wonderful sweetener for lattes.

> 1 tsp. honey
> ½ oz. hazelnut syrup
> 1 shot espresso
> steamed milk
> cinnamon for garnish

In an 8-ounce cup, combine honey, syrup and espresso. Fill cup with steamed milk, top with foam and sprinkle with cinnamon.

IRISH NUT LATTE

Servings: 1

If your milk is steamed too hot, flavored lattes may curdle. Be sure to keep the temperature just below 150°.

1 oz. Irish cream syrup

1 oz. hazelnut syrup

1 shot espresso

steamed milk

In an 8-ounce cup, combine syrups and espresso. Fill cup with steamed milk and top with foam.

VARIATIONS

- Use macadamia nut syrup instead of hazelnut.
- Use praline syrup instead of hazelnut.
- Add 1 oz. chocolate topping for a mocha.
- Use half and half instead of milk for a rich breve style.

CHOCOLATE MALT LATTE

Servings: 1

Use the powdered malt mix from your grocery store. It's usually available near the cocoa mix.

> 3 tsp. malt powder
> 1 oz. chocolate ice cream syrup
> 1 shot espresso
> steamed milk
> cocoa powder and a sprinkle of malt for garnish

In an 8-ounce cup, combine malt powder, syrup and espresso. Fill cup with steamed milk, top with foam and garnish with cocoa powder and a sprinkle of malt.

VARIATION

• Use chocolate malt syrup.

MANDARIN CHOCOLATE LATTE

Servings: 1

Chocolate, orange and coffee make a wonderful combination. Always add the flavors and syrups first; some syrups such as hazelnut and vanilla may curdle if added later.

1 oz. chocolate topping
1 oz. mandarindo syrup
1 shot espresso

steamed milk
orange-flavored whipped cream, optional
chocolate sprinkles for garnish

In an 8-ounce cup, combine topping, syrup and espresso. Fill cup with steamed milk, top with whipped cream if desired, and garnish with chocolate sprinkles.

VARIATIONS

- Use chocolate fudge syrup instead of chocolate topping.
- Use orange syrup or grand orange syrup instead of mandarindo.
- Use Grand Marnier liqueur instead of orange syrup.
- Garnish with an orange slice or twist.

HOT BUTTERED RUM BREVE

Servings: 1

If your espesso is too slow extracting (it should only take about 20 seconds), make sure the coffee is not ground too fine, tamped too lightly or you have too much in the basket.

1 oz. Swedish rum syrup
½ oz. vanilla syrup
1 shot espresso
steamed half and half
nutmeg for garnish

In an 8-ounce cup, combine syrups and espresso. Fill cup with steamed half and half, top with foam and sprinkle with nutmeg.

E. T.'S FAVORITE

Servings: 1

*In Steven Spielberg's movie **E.T.**, the little space creature enjoyed **Reese's Pieces** candies. This syrup makes a great latte. While experimenting for this book, we did try adding peanut butter to a latte — we didn't care for it, but others might.*

1 oz. chocolate peanut butter syrup
½ oz. chocolate topping

1 shot espresso
steamed milk

In an 8-ounce cup, combine syrup, topping and espresso. Fill cup with steamed milk and top with foam.

VARIATIONS

- Add ½ oz. banana syrup.
- Add ½ oz. strawberry, cherry or grape syrup for a P & B sandwich flavor!
- Add 2 tsp. honey.

MINT PATTY LATTE

Servings: 1

If you are using glass coffee mugs, be sure to place a spoon in the mug before pouring hot coffee to prevent breakage.

1 oz. chocolate fudge syrup
1 oz. peppermint syrup

1 shot espresso
steamed milk

In an 8-ounce cup, combine syrups and espresso. Fill cup with steamed milk and top with foam.

VARIATIONS

- Use crème de menthe syrup instead of peppermint.
- Use chocolate mint syrup instead of chocolate fudge.
- Use chocolate topping instead of chocolate fudge.
- Add a peppermint patty candy wedge on the edge of the cup.

RUM PRALINE BREVE

Servings: 1

Tastes like pecan pie with whipped cream in a cup.

>1 oz. rum syrup
>1 oz. praline syrup
>½ oz. hazelnut syrup
>1 shot espresso
>steamed half and half
>whipped cream

In an 8-ounce cup, combine syrups and espresso. Fill cup with steamed half and half and top with whipped cream.

TOFFEE COFFEE LATTE

Servings: 1

In Constantinople in the 16th century, failure to provide your wife with coffee was "grounds" for divorce!

1 oz. caramel syrup
½ oz. praline syrup
1 oz. chocolate syrup
1 shot espresso
steamed milk
finely chopped toffee for garnish, optional

In an 8-ounce cup, combine syrups and espresso. Fill cup with steamed milk, top with foam and garnish with finely chopped toffee, if desired.

BANANA FUDGE LATTE

Servings: 1

According to one espresso stand operator, she has a customer who regularly drinks SIX shots of espresso at a time!

1 oz. banana syrup
1 oz. chocolate fudge syrup
½ oz. vanilla syrup
2 shots espresso

steamed milk
chocolate whipped cream
sprinkles for garnish

In a 10-ounce cup, combine syrups and espresso. Fill with steamed milk, top with chocolate whipped cream and garnish with sprinkles.

VARIATIONS

- Add ½ oz. macadamia nut syrup instead of vanilla.
- Add ½ oz. hazelnut syrup instead of vanilla.

TROPICAL DELIGHT

Servings: 1

Flavors from the Islands combine in this latte.

1 oz. Swedish rum syrup
½ oz. coconut syrup
½ oz. macadamia nut syrup
1 shot espresso
steamed milk

In an 8-ounce cup, combine syrups and espresso. Fill with steamed milk and top with foam.

HUNGARIAN HAZELNUT BREVE

Servings: 1

A taste of old Vienna. Be sure to garnish with whipped cream and worry about the calories tomorrow!

1 oz. hazelnut syrup
½ oz. vanilla syrup
1 shot espresso
steamed half and half
whipped cream
shaved chocolate for garnish

In an 8-ounce cup, combine syrups and espresso. Fill cup with steamed half and half, top with whipped cream and garnish with shaved chocolate.

ICED LATTES

TROPICAL DELIGHT ICED LATTE

Servings: 1

Bananas are the most frequently eaten fruit in the United States. They are also the most digestible and the least expensive. Passion fruit may or may not have aphrodisiac properties (!) but it is really named for part of the plant's resemblance to the thorns in the crown worn by Christ during his crucifixion.

ice
1 shot espresso
2 oz. banana syrup

1 oz. passion fruit syrup
cold milk

Fill a 12-ounce glass with ice. Add espresso and syrups. Fill glass with cold milk.

VARIATIONS
- Add 1 oz. pineapple syrup.
- Add 1 oz. coconut syrup.
- Add 1 oz. guava syrup.

RED CACTUS ICED LATTE

Add a bit of rum or vodka if desired.

>ice
>1 shot espresso
>2 oz. raspberry syrup
>1 oz. kiwi syrup
>1 oz. lime syrup
>cold milk

Fill a 12-ounce glass with ice. Add espresso and syrups. Fill glass with cold milk. Stir to combine flavors.

GINGER PEAR ICED MOCHA

Servings: 1

You can use peach syrup instead of pear in this drink.

ice
1 shot espresso
1 oz. chocolate syrup
2 oz. pear syrup
1 oz. ginger syrup
cold milk

Fill a 12-ounce glass with ice. Add espresso and syrups. Fill glass with cold milk. Stir to combine flavors.

ACAPULCO MOCHA ICED LATTE

Servings: 1

You can use cream of coconut or coconut syrup in this drink.

> ice
> 1 shot espresso
> 1 oz. chocolate syrup
> 1 oz. orange syrup or grand orange syrup
> 1 oz. cream of coconut or coconut syrup
> cold milk

Fill a 12-ounce glass with ice, add espresso and syrups and fill with cold milk. Stir to combine flavors.

ICED MAI TAI LATTE

Servings: 1

What is better than a taste of the tropics on a hot day?

ice
1 shot espresso
1 oz. rum syrup
1 oz. orgeat syrup

1 oz. orange syrup
1 tbs. grenadine
1 tsp. lime juice
cold milk

Fill a 12-ounce glass with ice. Add espresso, syrups, grenadine and lime juice. Fill glass with cold milk. Stir to combine flavors.

VARIATION

• Use real rum instead of rum syrup.

MAPLE WALNUT ICED MOCHA

Servings: 1

Rich and satisfying for a quick pick-me-up drink.

ice
1 shot espresso
2 oz. maple nut syrup

1 oz. chocolate syrup
cold milk

Fill a 12-ounce glass with ice. Add espresso and syrups. Fill glass with cold milk. Stir to combine flavors.

VARIATIONS

- Use hazelnut syrup instead of maple nut.
- Use golden pecan syrup instead of maple nut.
- Use macadamia nut syrup instead of maple nut.

ICED RASPBERRY GUAVA LATTE

Servings: 1

Guavas are one of our favorite fruits. They are exceptionally high in vitamins and can be served in a variety of ways. At your next brunch try adding guava syrup or juice to champagne for a refreshing drink.

ice
1 shot espresso
2 oz. raspberry syrup

1 oz. guava syrup
cold milk

Fill a 12-ounce glass with ice. Add espresso and syrups. Fill glass with cold milk. Stir to combine flavors.

VARIATIONS

- Add 1 oz. banana syrup.
- Add 1 oz. peach syrup.

- Add 1 oz. passion fruit syrup.
- Add 1 oz. orgeat syrup.

ICED MELBA LATTE

Servings: 1

This one is a take-off from the popular dessert, Peach Melba.

ice
1 shot espresso
2 oz. peach syrup
1 oz. raspberry syrup
cold milk

Fill a 12-ounce glass with ice. Add espresso and syrups. Fill glass with cold milk. Stir to combine flavors.

TRADE WINDS ICED LATTE

Servings: 1

This unusual flavored iced drink is made with Tamarindo syrup from the Torani Company. Some people think it tastes like dates with a touch of lemon or apricot. Tamarinds are the fruit pods of a tropical tree. Two to six inches in size, they can be eaten fresh and served with rice or fish. The spicy pulp is also used in chutneys and curries.

ice
1 shot espresso
2 oz. Tamarindo syrup
1 tbs. lemon syrup
cold milk

Fill a 12-ounce glass with ice. Add espresso and syrups. Fill glass with cold milk. Stir to combine flavors.

ICED MOCHA MINT

Servings: 1

Fresh mint is so easy to grow in your garden or a planter. Use a sprig to garnish this refreshing drink.

ice
1 shot of espresso
1 oz. chocolate syrup
2 oz. crème de menthe syrup
1 oz. crème de cacao syrup
cold milk

Fill a 12-ounce glass with ice. Add espresso and syrups. Fill glass with cold milk. Stir to combine flavors.

CAPPUCCINOS AND MOCHAS

BASIC CAPPUCCINO

Servings: 1

This basic recipe can be infinitely varied to suit your personal taste.

2-3 oz. espresso
¾ cup foamed milk
flavoring of your choice

Pour a single shot of espresso in a cup. Use flavoring if desired. Add milk. A spoon used to scoop the foam from the pitcher is a big help. Enjoy.

FLAVORING IDEAS

amaretto	chocolate mint	crème de menthe	orange
banana	chocolate	coffee	grand orange
carmel	chocolate fudge	hazelnut	peppermint
cherry	coconut	Irish cream	vanilla
cinnamon	crème de cacao	macadamia nut	

ROCKY ROAD CAPPUCCINO

An ice cream favorite in a steaming cup!

> 1 oz. chocolate topping, such as Hershey's
> 1 oz. hazelnut syrup
> 2 shots espresso
> steamed milk
> miniature marshmallows
> cocoa for garnish

In a 12-ounce cup, combine syrups and espresso. Fill cup with steamed milk and top with foam. Add miniature marshmallows and a sprinkle of cocoa for garnish.

VARIATIONS

- Use chocolate syrup or chocolate fudge syrup.
- Use maple nut syrup or golden pecan syrup.

AMARETTO FUDGE CAPPUCCINO

Servings: 1

The most common error in brewing espresso is brewing too much coffee from the grounds.

1 oz. amaretto syrup
1 oz. chocolate fudge syrup
½ oz. almond syrup
2 shots espresso
steamed milk
chocolate whipped cream for garnish

In a 12-ounce cup, combine syrups and espresso. Fill cup with steamed milk, top with foam and garnish with chocolate whipped cream.

BLACK FOREST MOCHA CAPPUCCINO

Servings: 1

The tangy bing cherries, a bit of orange and a hint of cinnamon make this a wonderful combination.

1 oz. chocolate syrup
1 oz. bing cherry syrup
½ oz. grand orange syrup
2 shots espresso
fill with steamed milk
top with foam
freshly grated orange zest for garnish
cinnamon for garnish

In a 12-ounce cup, combine syrups and espresso. Fill with steamed milk and top with foam. Sprinkle with orange zest and dust with cinnamon.

CAPPUCCINO SUPREME

Servings: 1

Vary the liquor in this drink to suit your taste. Amaretto, Galliano, Frangelico and Kahlua are all delightful.

1 shot espresso
1 oz. amaretto
1 oz. brandy
steamed milk

In an 8-ounce cup, combine espresso, amaretto and brandy. Fill cup with steamed milk and top with foam.

CARAMEL APPLE CAPPUCCINO

Servings: 1

Just like a caramel apple but without the stick!

> 1 oz. apple syrup
> 1 oz. caramel syrup
> ½ oz. vanilla syrup
> 2 shots espresso
> steamed milk
> whipped cream
> vanilla powder for garnish

In a 12-ounce cup, combine syrups and espresso. Fill cup with steamed milk and top with whipped cream. Dust with vanilla powder.

GERMAN CHOCOLATE CAPPUCCINO

Servings: 1

Caramel, pecans and coconut combined in a cup!

1 oz. chocolate syrup
1 oz. caramel syrup
1 oz. coconut syrup
½ oz. praline syrup

2 shots espresso
steamed half and half
shaved chocolate for garnish

In a 12-ounce cup, combinne syrups and espresso. Fill cup with steamed half and half, top with foam and sprinkle with shaved chocolate.

VARIATIONS

- Use almond syrup instead of praline.
- Use hazelnut syrup instead of praline.

AMARETTO ALMOND CAPPUCCINO

Servings: 1

As Mae West once said, "Too much of a good thing is wonderful."

1 oz. amaretto syrup
1 oz. almond syrup
2 shots espresso
steamed milk
whipped cream
finely chopped toasted almonds for garnish, optional

In a 12-ounce cup, combine syrups and espresso. Fill cup with steamed milk and top with whipped ccream. Garnish with chopped almonds if desired.

THE GREAT ESCAPE

Servings: 1

When you want to get away from it all, sip one of these.

3 shots Bailey's Irish Cream
2 shots vodka
1 shot amaretto
1 shot espresso

Combine ingredients in a coffee mug.

KAHLUA MOUSSE BREVE

Servings: 1

Dessert in a cup. Use the chocolate whipped cream recipe on page 19.

> 1 oz. chocolate syrup
> 1 oz. Kahlua syrup
> 2 shots espresso
> steamed half and half
> chocolate whipped cream
> chocolate curls for garnish

In a 12-ounce cup, combine syrups and espresso. Fill cup with steamed half and half and top with chocolate whipped cream. Garnish with chocolate curls.

LA DOLCE VITA

Servings: 1

Ah, the sweet life — Italians enjoy flavoring their coffee drinks with licorice-flavored liqueurs.

1½ oz. anisette syrup
2 shots espresso
steamed milk
a twist of lemon for garnish

In a 12-ounce cup, combine syrup and espresso. Fill cup with steamed milk, top with foam and garnish with a twist of lemon.

VARIATION

• Use Sambucca syrup instead of anisette.

APPLE CINNAMON CAPPUCCINO

Servings: 1

Experts say that if your cappuccino foam is "dry" you should be able to stand a ice tea spoon in a 12-ounce cup and it won't fall over...

2 oz. apple syrup
½ oz. cinnamon syrup
2 shots espresso
steamed milk
cinnamon for garnish

In a 12-ounce cup, combine syrups and espresso. Fill cup with steamed milk, top with foam and sprinkle with cinnamon.

MACADAMIA FUDGE CAPPUCCINO

Servings: 1

Macadamia nuts are high in calories but high in nutrition. One sip of this drink and you'll feel justified whatever the case may be!

1 oz. chocolate fudge syrup
1 oz. macadamia nut syrup
2 shots espresso

steamed milk
whipped cream
cocoa powder for garnish

In a 12-ounce cup, combine syrups and espresso. Fill cup with steamed milk, top with whipped cream and sprinkle with cocoa powder.

VARIATIONS

- Add ½ oz. coconut syrup.
- Add ½ oz. banana syrup.

MEXICAN MOCHA CAPPUCCINO

Servings: 1

The ideal storage temperature for chocolate is 78°. If stored at temperatures too high, it gets a gray "bloom" on the chocolate. It detracts from the appearance, but it is harmless — just the fat content coming to the surface. Mexicans enjoy adding chocolate and cinnamon to their coffee drinks.

1 oz. chocolate syrup
1 oz. Kahlua syrup
2 shots espresso
steamed milk
cinnamon for garnish
cinnamon stick for garnish

In a 12-ounce cup, combine syrups and espresso. Fill cup with steamed milk, top with foam and sprinkle with cinnamon. Garnish with a cinnamon stick.

WHITE CHOCOLATE MACADAMIA CAPPUCCINO

Servings: 1

White chocolate isn't chocolate at all, but a combination of vegetable fat, coloring and flavoring. Finely chop it in the food processor using the steel blade.

1 oz. white chocolate, finely chopped
1½ oz. macadamia nut syrup
2 shots espresso
steamed milk
whipped cream
vanilla powder for garnish

In a 12-ounce cup, combine white chocolate, syrup and espresso. Fill cup with steamed milk, top with whipped cream and sprinkle with vanilla powder.

PINA COLADA MOCHA

Servings: 1

Chocolate comes from an evergreen tree of the genus Theobroma — meaning food of the gods.

1 oz. chocolate syrup
1 oz. coconut syrup
½ oz. pineapple syrup
2 shots espresso
steamed milk

In a 12-ounce cup, combine syrups and espresso. Fill cup with steamed milk and top with foam.

CHERRY AMARETTO MOCHA

Servings: 1

*On the back of a sweatshirt one day we saw the following **Single's Ad**:
"Single Americano seeks companionship and possible??! for winter commutes and
cafe encounters. Enjoys long sips along beach. Feels at home in a paper cup but
loves to dress up in a ceramic cup and saucer. Seeking double tall latte, any flavor,
who loves to go foamy and lidless. No decaf!! Refillable?! Maybe you can fill my
cup... Photo appreciated. PO Box 993."*

1 oz. chocolate syrup
1 oz. cherry syrup
1 oz. amaretto syrup

2 shots espresso
steamed milk
vanilla powder for garnish

In a 12-ounce cup, combine syrups and espresso. Fill cup with steamed milk, top
with foam and sprinkle with vanilla powder.

RASPBERRY TORTE

Servings: 1

Raspberries come from the species RUBUS and are related to blackberries, loganberries and boysenberries. They are small and tart and come in four different colors: red, yellow or amber, purple and black. Fresh raspberry season is all too short, so enjoy them anytime in this delicious drink.

1 oz. raspberry syrup
½ oz. crème de cacao syrup

2 shots espresso
steamed milk

In a 12-ounce cup, combine syrups and espresso. Fill cup with steamed milk and top with foam.

VARIATIONS

- Use chocolate syrup to coat the bottom of the cup.
- Use real crème de cacao liqueur.
- Use half and half for a richer breve style.

RASPBERRY TORTE BREVE

Servings: 1

Rich, warm and wonderful.

        1 oz. chocolate syrup
        1 oz. raspberry syrup
        ½ oz. crème de cacao syrup
        1 shot espresso
        steamed half and half

In a 12-ounce cup, combine syrups and espresso. Fill cup with steamed half and half.

STRAWBERRY AMARETTO MOCHA

Servings: 1

When Christie studied at the Cordon Bleu in London, one of the culinary tricks she learned was to add a tiny bit of finely ground pepper to crushed strawberries to bring out the flavor. It sounds crazy, but try it sometime! We do NOT advise putting pepper in a cappuccino!

1 oz. chocolate syrup
1 oz. strawberry syrup
1 oz. amaretto syrup
2 shots espresso
steamed milk
vanilla powder for garnish

In a 12-ounce cup, combine syrups and espresso. Fill cup with steamed milk, top with foam and sprinkle with vanilla powder.

TANGERINE RASPBERRY CAPPUCCINO

Servings: 1

*There is a tangerine-flavored liqueur on the market called Mandarin Napoleon.
The flavored syrup works well with this recipe.*

1 oz. chocolate syrup
1 oz. mandarindo syrup
½ oz. raspberry syrup
2 shots espresso
steamed milk
orange-flavored whipped cream
a strip of orange peel for garnish

In a 12-ounce cup, combine syrups and espresso. Fill cup with steamed milk and
top with whipped cream. Garnish with a strip of orange peel.

STEAMERS

CHOCOLATE VELVET 78
HOT NUTTY IRISH. 79
ALMOND APRICOT STEAMER 80
CHOCOLATE STEAMER 81
PEPPERMINT STEAMER. 82
APPLE COBBLER STEAMER 83
SNOW CAP 84
ALMOND MOO 85

With all of the delicious flavors of syrups available, it's fun to create your own special drinks. We find them to have a soporific effect and enjoy sipping a cozy steamer while reading in bed.

CHOCOLATE VELVET

Servings: 1

Chocolate has always been associated with passion.

> 1 oz. chocolate syrup
> 1 oz. rum syrup
> steamed milk

In a 8-ounce cup, combine syrups. Fill cup with steamed milk.

HOT NUTTY IRISH

You'll go nuts over this combination!

> 1 oz. Irish cream syrup
> 1 oz. hazelnut syrup
> steamed milk

In a 8-ounce cup, combine syrups. Fill cup with steamed milk.

ALMOND APRICOT STEAMER

Servings: 1

Apricot and almond complement each other in many delicious foods. Most of the apricots grown in the U.S. come from the San Joaquin Valley in California.

1 oz. almond syrup
1 oz. apricot syrup
steamed milk

In an 8-ounce cup, combine syrups and fill with steamed milk.

VARIATIONS

• Use 1 oz. peach, raspberry, cherry or strawberry syrup instead of apricot.

CHOCOLATE STEAMER

Servings: 1

Drinking chocolate beverages began with the Aztecs.

2 oz. chocolate syrup
steamed milk

Into an 8-ounce cup, pour syrup and fill with steamed milk.

VARIATIONS

- Use chocolate fudge, chocolate malt, or chocolate mint instead of chocolate syrup.

PEPPERMINT STEAMER

Servings: 1

You're off to sweet dreams when you've sipped one of these.

2 oz. peppermint syrup
steamed milk

Into an 8-ounce cup, pour syrup and fill with steamed milk.

VARIATION

• Use crème de menthe syrup instead of peppermint.

APPLE COBBLER STEAMER

Servings: 1

*It seems strange to see signs on Chinese restaurants in Seattle: **Espresso Served Here.***

1 oz. apple syrup
½ oz. walnut syrup
steamed milk
cinnamon for garnish

In an 8-ounce cup, combine syrups and fill with steamed milk. Sprinkle with cinnamon.

SNOW CAP

Servings: 1

Seattle is "Latte Land." One popular bumper sticker warns: **Caution — I brake for lattes.**

2 oz. vanilla syrup
steamed milk

Into an 8-ounce cup, pour syrup and fill with steamed milk.

VARIATIONS

- Add ½ oz. caramel syrup.
- Add ½ oz. butterscotch syrup
- Add ½ oz. macadamia nut syrup.

ALMOND MOO

One of our favorite bedtime soothers.

2 oz. almond syrup
steamed milk

Into an 8-ounce cup, pour syrup and fill with steamed milk.

COFFEE WITH SPIRIT

FRENCH ROYALE

Servings: 1

This delicious cold drink is made with Chambord liqueur. Chambord was first produced in France during the time of King Louis XIV and is made from small black raspberries (framboises), other selected fruits and honey.

1 oz. Chambord
1 oz. espresso
1 oz. heavy cream
½ cup crushed ice

Combine Chambord, espresso, cream and ½ cup of crushed ice in a blender and mix on high speed for about 25 seconds. Pour into a large cocktail glass and serve.

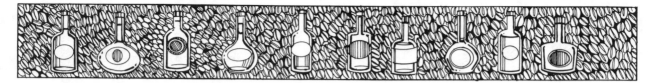

CAFÉ VIENNESE

Servings: 1

Coffee and chocolate is a classic flavor combination that will always be popular. This recipe combines espresso, Kahlua and crème de cacao for a delicious hot drink.

1 oz. Kahlua
1 oz. crème de cacao
2 oz. espresso
4 oz. hot water (or hot chocolate)
sweetened whipped cream

Pour Kahlua and crème de cacao into a 10- to 12-ounce mug. Add espresso and hot water. Top with sweetened whipped cream.

VARIATION

- If you are a real chocoholic, use hot chocolate instead of hot water and use shaved chocolate to garnish the whipped cream.

CAFÉ BAVARIAN

Servings: 1

Those of you who like the flavored international coffees will enjoy this.

½ oz. peppermint schnapps
1 oz. Kahlua
2 oz. espresso
4 oz. hot water
sweetened whipped cream

Pour peppermint schnapps and Kahlua into an 10- to 12-ounce mug. Add espresso and hot water. Top with sweetened whipped cream.

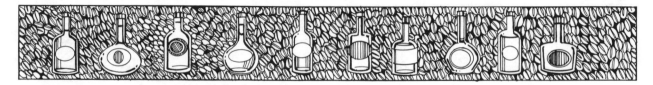

CAFÉ CARIBBEAN

Servings: 1

If you want to add a touch of elegance for yourself or guests, first moisten the rim of your coffee mug with lemon juice and dip it in granulated sugar.

1 oz. dark rum
1 oz. Tia Maria
2 oz. espresso
4 oz. hot water
whipped cream

Pour rum and Tia Maria into an 8- to 12-ounce mug. Add espresso and hot water. Top with sweetened whipped cream.

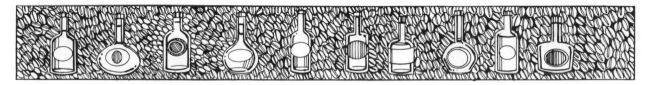

CAFÉ AMARETTO

Servings: 1

Put your feet up in front of a cozy fire and relax with one of these.

> 1 oz. amaretto
> 2 oz. espresso
> 4 oz. hot water
> 2 heaping tablespoons of coffee ice cream
> allspice

Pour amaretto into a heat-resistant 8- to 12-ounce mug. Add espresso and hot water and top with softened coffee ice cream. Sprinkle ice cream with allspice. Add a cozy fire and you're done.

WEST INDIES TRADE WIND

Servings: 1

We tried a variation of this drink when we visited the Caribbean on a vacation and loved it. Christie favors Meyer's Rum.

1 oz. dark rum
1 oz. amaretto
2 oz. espresso
4 oz. hot water
sweetened whipped cream
cherry for garnish, optional

Pour rum and amaretto into a large cup or mug. Add espresso and hot water. Top with sweetened whipped cream. Garnish with a cherry if desired.

THE IRISH MOUNTIE

Servings: 1

If Dudley Doright were a drinking man, I imagine he would go for one of these. It combines Yukon Jack, Bailey's Irish Cream and espresso for a drink that's sure to keep anyone warm and awake during cold winter evenings.

1 oz. Yukon Jack
1 oz. Bailey's Irish Cream
2 oz. espresso
4 oz. hot water
sweetened whipped cream

Pour Yukon Jack and Bailey's into a 10- to 12-ounce mug. Add espresso and hot water. Top with sweetened whipped cream.

CAFÉ BRÛLOT

Servings: 4

Café Brûlot hails from the bayous of Louisiana where it is rumored to have been invented by Captain Lafitte himself. The preparation is fun and will provide some entertainment for your guests. Final preparation should be in a darkened room for the best effect.

1 small orange
10 whole cloves
2 cinnamon sticks
5 sugar cubes
zest of 1 large orange
zest of 1 large lemon
½ cup brandy
¼ cup Cointreau
16 oz. hot espresso
(Hint: Keep the espresso in a thermos bottle until ready to be used.)

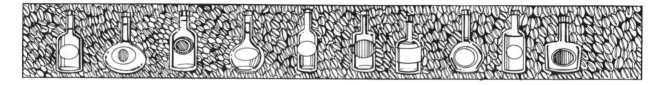

Have ready a deep, elegant bowl, serving tray, and demitasse cups suitable for serving guests. Stud orange with whole cloves and set aside. Next, use a zester to remove outer layer of orange and lemon and place combined zest in the deep bowl along with cinnamon sticks and sugar cubes. Heat ½ cup brandy in a small saucepan, but do not let it boil. When heated, pour brandy over ingredients in bowl. Place bowl on a tray and bring studded orange, bowl and tray, a large ladle and your espresso to your serving table.

Ignite brandy mixture and ladle it over spices until sugar melts. Pour espresso into bowl. Fill ladle with ¼ cup Cointreau. Carefully place orange into ladle, ignite liqueur, and carefully lower ladle into Café Brûlot, allowing orange to float on the surface. Ladle Café Brûlot into demitasse cups and serve to your guests, who no doubt will be suitably impressed.

CAFÉ PARISIAN

Servings: 1

This is another classic flavor combination. This recipe combines espresso, Grand Marnier and brandy for an interesting hot drink for a tranquil moment in your life.

1 oz. brandy
1 oz. Grand Marnier
2 oz. espresso
4 oz. hot water
sweetened whipped cream

Pour brandy and Grand Marnier into an 10- to 12-ounce mug. Add espresso and hot water. Top with sweetened whipped cream. Garnish with orange peel or with the zest of an orange.

THE MEXICAN STANDOFF

Servings: 1

Share one of these with your favorite señor or señorita.

> 1 oz. tequila
> 1 oz. Kahlua
> 2 oz. espresso
> 4 oz. hot water
> sweetened whipped cream
> cocoa powder for garnish

Pour tequila and Kahlua into a 10- to 12-ounce mug. Add espresso and hot water. Top with sweetened whipped cream. Dust whipped cream with cocoa powder for added effect.

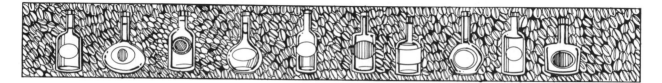

ESPRESSO NUDGE

This is the espresso version of the familiar coffee nudge.

1 oz. brandy
1 oz. crème de cacao
2 oz. espresso
4 oz. hot water
sweetened whipped cream

Pour brandy and crème de cacao into a 10- to 12-ounce mug. Add espresso and hot water. Top with sweetened whipped cream.

FOREVER IRISH

Servings: 1

St. Patrick himself would like one of these.

1 oz. Irish whiskey
1 oz. Bailey's Irish Cream
2 oz. espresso
4 oz. hot water
2 tsp. turbinado sugar
sweetened whipped cream

Pour Irish whiskey and Bailey's Irish Cream into a 10- to 12-ounce mug. Add espresso and hot water. Add turbinado sugar and stir until dissolved. Top with sweetened whipped cream.

CHERRY RUM HEATER

Servings: 1

Perfect in front of a fire on a cold winter night.

1 oz. cherry-flavored brandy
1 oz. light rum
2 oz. espresso
4 oz. hot water
sweetened whipped cream

Pour brandy and rum into a 10- to 12-ounce mug. Add espresso and hot water. Top with sweetened whipped cream. Garnish with a stemmed cherry.

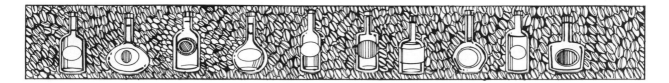

NEW ORLEANS COOLER

Servings: 1

This is simple, quick and oh, so good!

1 oz. bourbon
1 oz. praline syrup
2 oz. espresso
6-8 oz. cold milk
½ cup crushed ice

Combine bourbon, praline syrup, espresso, and milk in a shaker with ½ cup crushed ice and shake well. Strain into a 12-ounce tumbler.

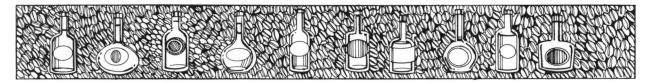

CABO COOLER

Servings: 1

*We visited Cabo San Lucas a couple of years ago where we were served a variation of this in the hotel lounge. I don't recall what they called it, but **Cabo Cooler** seems appropriate.*

1 oz. Kahlua
1 oz. dark rum
4 oz. espresso
2 oz. heavy cream
1 tsp. sugar
½ cup crushed ice

Combine Kahlua, rum, espresso, and cream in a shaker with ½ cup crushed ice and shake well. Strain into a 12-ounce tumbler.

ROCKY ROAD

Servings: 1

Frangelico is a popular liqueur with the taste of toasted hazelnuts.

1 oz. Frangelico
1 oz. crème de cacao
2 oz. espresso
4 oz. hot chocolate
miniature marshmallows

Combine Frangelico, crème de cacao, espresso, and hot chocolate in a 10- to 12-ounce mug and top with miniature marshmallows.

WHITE RUSSIAN

Servings: 1

An all-time favorite. Kahlua is derived from a sugar cane alcohol base.

1 oz. Kahlua
1 oz. vodka
4 oz. chilled espresso
4 oz. half and half
sugar to taste
½ cup crushed ice

Combine Kahlua, vodka, espresso, and cream in a shaker with ½ cup crushed ice and shake well. Taste and add sugar as needed. Strain into a 12-ounce tumbler.

JAMAICA JOY

Servings: 1

Add a bit of joy to your evening.

1 oz. dark rum
4 oz. espresso
4 oz. half and half
carbonated water
sugar to taste

Combine rum, espresso and half and half. Chill until cold. Pour into a tall glass filled with ice and top with carbonated water. Add sugar to taste. Stir with a long spoon or a straw.

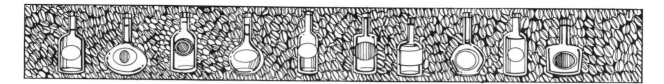

VELVET HAMMER

Servings: 1

The name says it all.

1 oz. vodka
1 oz. crème de cacao
2 oz. espresso
6 oz. half and half
sugar to taste
½ cup crushed ice

Combine vodka, crème de cacao, espresso and half and half into a shaker with ½ cup of ice and shake well. Pour into a tall glass. Add sugar to taste.

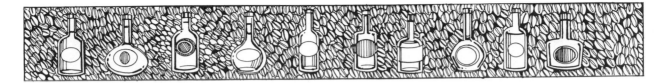

GRASSHOPPER

Servings: 1

Smooth and so refreshing!

1 oz. vodka
1 oz. white crème de menthe
1 oz. white crème de cacao
1 oz. half and half
4 oz. chilled espresso
½ cup crushed ice

Combine vodka, crème de menthe, crème de cacao, espresso, half and half, and crushed ice in a blender and mix until smooth. Pour into a tall chilled glass.

RESTLESS IN RENTON

Servings: 1

*After seeing the popular movie, **Sleepless in Seattle**, we decided to name a coffee drink after our town, thus **Restless in Renton**. Although we must confess, after one of these we go right to sleep.*

2 oz. Kahlua
2 oz. brandy
1 shot espresso
5 oz. half and half
sweetened whipped cream

Combine Kahlua, brandy, espresso, and hot half and half in a 10- to 12-ounce mug and top with whipped cream.

HOLIDAY SPECIALS

VALENTINE'S DAY

Servings: 1

Share one of these delightful chocolate cherry cappuccinos with your sweetheart this February 14th.

2 shots espresso
1 oz. chocolate syrup

1 oz. cherry syrup
steamed milk

In a 12-ounce cup, combine espresso and syrups. Fill cup with steamed milk and top with foam.

VARIATIONS

- Add ½ oz. almond syrup or amaretto syrup.
- Use half and half instead of milk for a richer breve style.
- Use chocolate fudge syrup.
- Top with whipped cream and a dusting of cocoa.

ST. PATRICK'S DAY

Servings: 1

Top this Shamrock special with whipped cream tinted green with a bit of food coloring.

1 shot espresso
1 oz. chocolate syrup
1 oz. crème de menthe syrup

steamed milk
whipped cream, tinted pale green

In an 8-ounce cup, combine espresso and syrups. Fill cup with steamed milk and top with tinted whipped cream.

VARIATIONS

- Use 1 oz. chocolate mint syrup.
- Add ½ oz. Irish cream syrup.
- Use crème de menth liqueur.

EASTER

Servings: 1

This rich cappuccino is reminiscent of those wonderful eggs found in your Easter basket.

2 shots espresso
1 oz. chocolate fudge syrup
1 oz. grand orange syrup
steamed milk

In a 12-ounce cup, combine espresso and syrups. Fill cup with steamed milk and top with foam.

MOTHER'S DAY

Servings: 1

What mother wouldn't enjoy this special drink on her special day?

2 shots espresso
1½ oz. strawberry syrup
½ oz. vanilla syrup
steamed half and half
vanilla powder for garnish
1 whole fresh strawberry for garnish

In a 12-ounce cup, combine espresso and syrups. Fill cup with steamed half and half, top with foam and sprinkle with vanilla powder. Garnish with a strawberry.

FATHER'S DAY

Servings:

Put Dad in his favorite hammock or easy chair and bring him one of these cool refreshers.

ice
1 shot espresso
1 oz. chocolate syrup
1 oz. peppermint syrup
cold milk
peppermint stick for garnish

Fill a 16-ounce glass with ice. Add espresso and syrups. Fill glass with cold milk and garnish with a peppermint stick.

4TH OF JULY

Servings: 1

Red, white and blue and tasting glorious!

ice
2 oz. blueberry syrup
1 oz. raspberry syrup
½ oz. strawberry syrup
8 oz. soda water
1 oz. half and half

Fill a 12-ounce glass with ice. Add syrups, soda and half and half. Stir with a spoon or straw to combine flavors.

HALLOWEEN

Servings: 1

When the neighborhood goblins have finished their tricks, relax with one of these.

        1 oz. chocolate syrup
        1 oz. orange syrup
        1 shot espresso
        steamed milk
        orange-flavored whipped cream
        cocoa for garnish

In a 12-ounce cup, combine syrups and espresso. Fill the cup with steamed milk and dust with cocoa.

THANKSGIVING

Servings: 1

Enjoying this latte with loved ones is something to be thankful for!

1 oz. apple syrup
½ oz. cinnamon syrup
2 tsp. honey
1 shot espresso
steamed milk
whipped cream
cinnamon for garnish
cinnamon stick for garnish

In an 8-ounce cup, combine syrups, honey and espresso. Fill cup with stemed milk and top with whipped cream. Garnish with sprinkles of cinnamon and a cinnamon stick.

HOLIDAY EGGNOG LATTE

Servings: 1

Commercially prepared eggnog is just wonderful steamed and served as a latte. It thickens as it stands, so only prepare enough for one latte at a time.

1 shot espresso   nutmeg for garnish
5 oz. eggnog, steamed

Pour espresso into an 8-ounce cup. Add steamed eggnog, top with foam and sprinkle with nutmeg.

VARIATIONS

- Add 1 oz. chocolate syrup for a mocha eggnog.
- Add 1 oz. Swedish rum syrup.
- Add 1 oz. liquor of your choice, such as brandy, rum or whiskey.
- Add 1 oz. liqueur of your choice, such as crème de cacao, Kahlua or Frangelico.
- Add ½ oz. fruit syrup such as apricot or peach.

COFFEE FOR A CROWD

COFFEE PUNCH

Servings: 4

Milk punches are traditional in the South. Try this creamy rich punch at your next party. For a change of pace use chocolate ice cream instead of vanilla.

1 gallon strong brewed coffee, chilled
¾ cup sugar
1 tbs. vanilla
1 gallon vanilla ice cream, softened
1 pint cream, whipped
freshly grated nutmeg for garnish

In a large punch bowl, stir together coffee, sugar and vanilla until sugar is dissolved. Add ice cream by the spoonfuls. Gently fold in whipped cream and sprinkle with nutmeg.

EGGNOG PUNCH

Servings: 24

This is a wonderful drink to serve at holiday time.

1 quart brewed coffee, chilled
1 quart commercial eggnog
1 quart eggnog ice cream, softened
8 oz. Kahlua
freshly grated nutmeg for garnish

In a large punch bowl, combine coffee and eggnog. Stir in ice cream by the spoonsful. Add Kahlua and sprinkle with nutmeg. Ladle into cups to serve.

MARDI GRAS PUNCH

Servings: 12

Careful, this one is smooth but it will sneak up on you!

> 1 quart bourbon
> 6 cups brewed espresso
> 1 pint half and half
> 1 cup amaretto
> 1 quart softened ice cream:
>   vanilla, chocolate or coffee

Combine bourbon, espresso, cream and amaretto. Chill until serving. To serve, pour mixture into a large punchbowl and spoon in softened ice cream. Ladle into punch cups.

AMARETTO CAFÉ

A wonderful drink to sip by the fire after a day on the slopes.

2 oz. semi sweet chocolate,
  finely chopped
2 oz. unsweetened chocolate,
  finely chopped
⅓ cup sugar
3 tbs. brown sugar

2 cups half and half
1 cup amaretto
4 shots espresso
steamed milk
1 cup whipped cream
2 tbs. grated semi sweet chocolate

Combine chocolates, sugars and half and half in a heavy saucepan and simmer until chocolate is melted and sugar is dissolved. Cool. Add amaretto and refrigerate until serving. Before serving, pour ¼ of the mixture into each coffee cup. Add 1 shot of espresso to each cup and fill with steamed milk. Top with whipped cream and chocolate shavings.

MILLIONAIRE'S MOCHA

Servings: 4

So rich, it's not for calorie counters.

> 4 oz. German sweet chocolate
> 1 can (14 oz) sweetened condensed milk
> 1 cup heavy cream, whipped
> 4 cups espresso

Melt chocolate with condensed milk in the top of the double boiler until smooth. Cool. Fold in whipped cream and refrigerate until serving. To serve, place one quarter of the mixture in a cup and fill with espresso.

VARIATIONS

- Add one shot of Bailey's Irish Cream, Grand Marnier, amaretto, Kahlua, Galliano, brandy or Southern Comfort to each serving.

RICH AND FAMOUS EGGNOG

Servings: 12

Unbelievably rich and sinfully good. Always be cautious when using raw egg yolks. Be sure your eggs are very fresh and keep them refrigerated until serving.

6 egg yolks
½ tsp. cinnamon
1 tsp. vanilla extract
pinch of salt
2 (10 oz.) cans evaporated milk

2 (12 oz.) cans cream of coconut
1 (14 oz.) can sweetened condensed
 milk
1 fifth white rum
12 cups cold coffee

Using an electric mixer, combine egg yolks, cinnamon and salt until smooth. Stir in evaporated milk, cream of coconut and condensed milk until smooth. Store in the refrigerator in a covered container. Just before serving, pour mixture into a large punch bowl and add rum and cold coffee. Mix well. Sprinkle top with a dusting of cinnamon.

ICED TURKISH CAFÉ AU LAIT

The cardamom pods add unusual flavor to this refreshing drink.

2 cups milk
2 cups half and half
¼ cup sugar
12 whole cardamom pods, crushed
4 cups strong brewed coffee, chilled

In a small saucepan combine milk, half and half, sugar and caradamom pods. Heat to boiling and stir until sugar is dissolved. Cool. Strain through cheesecloth and add coffee. Refrigerate until cold. To serve, pour over an ice cube in a stemmed goblet.

BRANDIED MOCHA FRAPPE

Servings: 8

This makes a nice dessert for a dinner party served in pretty cups.

1 pint coffee ice cream
½ cup brandy
½ cup vodka
⅓ cup crème de cacao liqueur
⅓ cup coffee syrup

Combine all ingredients in a blender or food processor until smooth. Pour into cups. Garnish with whipped cream and chocolate covered coffee beans.

ITALIAN CREAM SODAS

Although Italian cream sodas do not contain coffee, we thought we would be remiss not to include recipes for these refreshing drinks in our book. So many of the syrups you might have on hand to make lattes and cappuccinos are wonderful in these drinks. Some of the fruit-flavored syrups which are not particularly compatible with espresso, such as grape, kiwi, lime and watermelon, are perfect for Italian sodas. In fact, once our nine-year-old discovered raspberry Italian sodas it was hard getting him to go back to soda pop.

ITALIAN CREAM SODAS: BASIC RECIPE

Servings: 1

Vary this basic recipe with some of the flavors we suggest, or your own ideas.

ice
2 oz. flavored syrup
soda water

1 oz. half and half
whipped cream, optional

Fill a 16-ounce glass with ice. Add syrup, soda water and half and half. Stir with a tall spoon or a straw to combine flavors. Top with whipped cream if desired.

FLAVORS TO TRY

blueberry	orange	pineapple	cranberry
blackberry	lemon	raspberry	kiwi
boysenberry	lime	strawberry	grape
bing cherry	melon	peach	root beer
cherry	peach	passion fruit	watermelon
apricot			

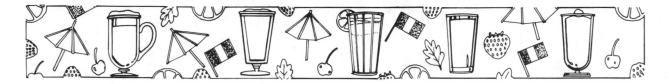

BANANA CREAM PIE

Servings: 1

Tastes just like its name.

> ice
> 1½ oz. banana syrup
> ½ oz. vanilla syrup
> dash of hazelnut syrup
> 8 oz. soda water
> 1 oz. half and half

Fill a 16-ounce glass with ice. Add syrups, soda water and half and half. Stir with a tall spoon or a straw to combine flavors.

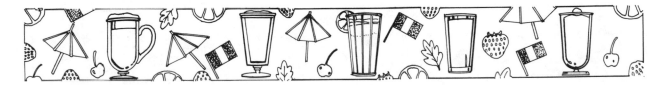

PEACH FUZZ

Guaranteed to win raves.

ice
2 oz. peach syrup
½ oz. coconut syrup
½ oz. orange syrup
soda water
1 oz. half and half
whipped cream, optional

Fill a 16-ounce glass with ice. Add syrups, soda water and half and half. Stir with a tall spoon or a straw to combine flavors. Top with whipped cream if desired.

BERRY BLITZ

Servings: 1

This tastes almost like berry cobbler.

ice
2 oz. berry syrup
1 oz. vanilla syrup

soda water
1 oz. half and half
whipped cream, optional

Fill a 16-ounce glass with ice. Add syrups, soda water and half and half. Stir with a tall spoon or a straw to combine flavors. Top with whipped cream if desired.

VARIATIONS

- Use blueberry syrup.
- Use blackberry syrup.
- Use boysenberry syrup.

SLICE OF SUMMER

Servings: 1

Enjoy after a day at the beach.

>ice
>2 oz. watermelon syrup
>1 oz. raspberry syrup
>soda water
>1 oz. half and half
>whipped cream, optional

Fill a 16-ounce glass with ice. Add syrups, soda water and half and half. Stir with a tall spoon or a straw to combine flavors. Top with whipped cream if desired.

VARIATIONS

• Use 1 oz. strawberry syrup instead of raspberry.

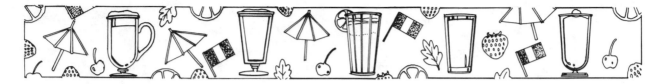

ALOHA SODA

The taste of the tropics in a glass. Experiment and use different proportions of the syrups to suit your taste.

> ice
> 1 oz. mango syrup
> 1 oz. coconut syrup
> 1 oz. guava syrup
> soda water
> 1 oz. half and half

Fill a 16-ounce glass with ice. Add syrups, soda water and half and half. Stir with a tall spoon or a straw to combine flavors.

VARIATIONS

• Add passion fruit, pineapple, orange, ginger or lime syrups.

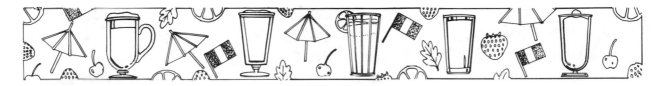

CREAMSICLE

Use orange, strawberry or raspberry syrup to create this treat.

ice
2 oz. orange syrup
½ oz. vanilla syrup
soda water
1 oz. half and half
whipped cream, optional

Fill a 16-ounce glass with ice. Add syrups, soda water and half and half. Stir with a tall spoon or a straw to combine flavors.

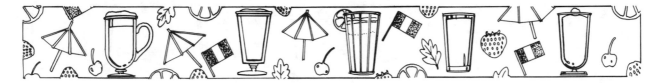

IRISH ROSE

Servings: 1

A romantic name for a refreshing drink.

ice
1½ oz. Irish cream syrup
1 oz. raspberry syrup
8 oz. soda water
1 oz. half and half

Fill a 16-ounce glass with ice. Add syrups, soda water and half and half. Stir with a tall spoon or a straw to combine flavors.

KEY LIME PIE

Servings: 1

A taste treat from Florida.

ice
2 oz. lime syrup
1 oz. vanilla syrup
soda water
1 oz. half and half
whipped cream

Fill a 16-ounce glass with ice. Add syrups, soda water and half and half. Stir with a tall spoon or a straw to combine flavors. Top with whipped cream.

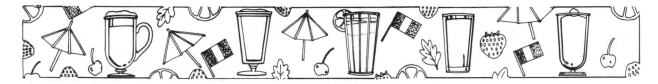

CRANBERRY GRAPE

Servings: 1

A taste of Cape Cod in a glass.

ice
2 oz. cranberry syrup
1 oz. grape syrup
soda water
1 oz. half and half
whipped cream, optional

Fill a 16-ounce glass with ice. Add syrups, soda water and half and half. Stir with a tall spoon or a straw to combine flavors. Top with whipped cream if desired.

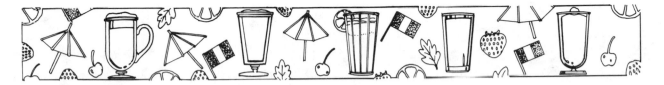

KIWI KISS

Servings: 1

Kiwi fruit originally came from New Zealand and in recent years have become very popular in the United States. They are brown and hairy on the outside, beautifully patterned and green inside.

ice
2 oz. kiwi syrup
1 oz. lime syrup
soda water
1 oz. half and half
whipped cream, optional

Fill a 16-ounce glass with ice. Add syrups, soda water and half and half. Stir with a tall spoon or a straw to combine flavors. Top with whipped cream if desired.

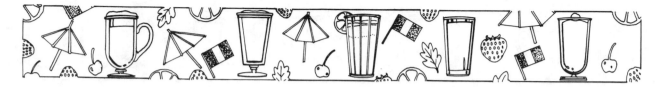

O. J. SPECIAL

Servings: 1

So refreshing and good for you too.

ice
2 oz. vanilla syrup
2 oz. half and half cream
fresh orange juice

Fill a 16-ounce glass with ice. Add syrup and half and half. Fill with fresh orange juice. Stir with a tall spoon or a straw to combine flavors.

TUTTI FRUITTI

Experiment using different combinations of fruit syrups to create your own special drink.

ice
1 oz. banana syrup
1 oz. pineapple syrup
½ oz. orange syrup
½ oz. strawberry syrup

½ oz. peach syrup
soda water
1 oz. half and half
whipped cream, optional

Fill a 16-ounce glass with ice. Add syrups, soda water and half and half. Stir with a tall spoon or a straw to combine flavors. Top with whipped cream if desired.

ITALIAN CREAM SODAS 141

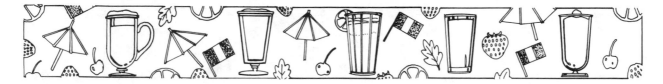

HARVEY WALLBANGER

Servings: 1

A popular drink minus the alcohol.

> ice
> 2 oz. orange syrup
> $\frac{1}{2}$ oz. anisette syrup
> soda water
> 1 oz. half and half
> whipped cream, optional

Fill a 16-ounce glass with ice. Add syrups, soda water and half and half. Stir with a tall spoon or a straw to combine flavors. Top with whipped cream if desired.

VARIATIONS

• Use $\frac{1}{2}$ oz. grenadine syrup instead of anisette to make a "Sunset."

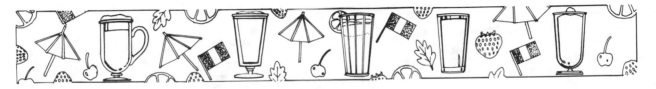

PEPPERMINT TWIST

Servings: 1

This is very refreshing on a hot afternoon. Garnish with a peppermint stick and a sprig of mint.

1½ oz. peppermint syrup
8 oz. soda water
1 oz. milk

Fill a 12-ounce glass with ice. Add syrup, soda water and milk. Stir to combine.

VARIATIONS

• Add ½ oz. chocolate, chocolate mint or chocolate fudge syrup.

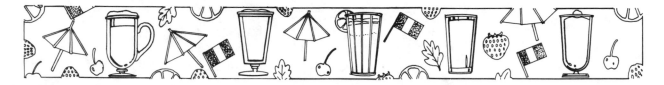

RED LICORICE

Servings: 1

Something a bit different in a drink!

> ice
> 2 oz. raspberry syrup
> 1 oz. licorice syrup
> soda water
> 1 oz. half and half
> whipped cream, optional

Fill a 16-ounce glass with ice. Add syrups, soda water and half and half. Stir with a tall spoon or a straw to combine flavors. Top with whipped cream if desired.

SUMMER SLUSH

Servings: 1

You can use almost any fruit flavored syrup or combination to create refreshing Summer drinks. Kids love them!

1 cup ice cubes
2 oz. watermelon syrup

Blend until smooth and pour into a glass.

OTHER SYRUPS TO TRY

blackberry	grape	passion fruit	rootbeer
blueberry	kiwi	peach	strawberry
boysenberry	lemon	orange	watermelon
cherry	lime	pineapple	
cranberry	orange	raspberry	

SOMETHING DIFFERENT: FRAPPES, SHAKES AND SODAS

BASIC FRAPPE

Servings: 1

Experiment with different flavors and combinations until you find your favorites.

ice
3 oz. flavored syrup
2 oz. half and half

Fill a blender half full with ice and add flavored syrup. Add half and half cream and blend until smooth. Here are some ideas to try:

apricot	kiwi
blackberry	lime
boysenberry	peach
cherry	raspberry
grape	strawberry

MOCHA FRAPPE

Servings: 1

So cooling on a hot summer day.

ice
1 shot espresso
3 oz. coffee syrup
2 oz. half and half

Fill a blender half full of ice. Add espresso, syrup and half and half. Blend until smooth.

HAWAIIAN PARADISE

Servings: 1

Using cream of coconut in this drink gives it richness. Coconuts have over 360 uses: 200 of them are in foods.

ice
1 shot espresso
2 tbs. cream of coconut
1 oz. chocolate syrup
1 oz. macadamia nut syrup
2 oz. half and half

Fill a blender half full with ice. Add espresso, cream of coconut, syrups and half and half. Blend until smooth.

VARIATION

• Use 1 oz. coconut syrup instead of cream of coconut.

THE VAGABOND

For centuries coconuts have had the reputation of being vagabonds. Explorers have carried them along for hundreds of years, using their meat for nourishment and their liquid for survival.

ice
1 shot espresso
2 tbs. cream of coconut
2 oz. pineapple syrup
1 oz. rum syrup or rum
2 oz. half and half

Fill a blender half full with ice. Add espresso, cream of coconut, syrups and half and half. Blend until smooth.

VARIATION

• Use 1 oz. coconut syrup instead of cream of coconut.

RAZZLE DAZZLE

Servings: 1

Loaded with flavor...

ice
1 shot espresso
1 oz. raspberry syrup
½ oz. almond syrup
2 oz. half and half

Fill a blender half full of ice. Add espresso, syrups and half and half. Blend until smooth.

SUNRISE SMOOTHIE

Whenever your bananas get too ripe, just throw them in the freezer, skins and all. To use, thaw briefly and peel. Cut into inch-chunks while still frozen. They add delicious flavor and texture to frappes and shakes.

        ice
        1 shot espresso
        1 frozen banana, cut in chunks
        1 oz. vanilla syrup
        2 oz. half and half

Fill a blender half full with ice. Add espresso, banana, syrup and half and half. Blend until smooth.

COFFEE SHAKE

Servings: 1

Tom loves coffee ice cream, so this is his favorite. He says it's guaranteed to jump-start your heart!

2 oz. Kahlua or coffee syrup
1 shot espresso
1 cup milk
1 scoop coffee ice cream

In a blender, process Kahlua, espresso, milk and ice cream. Blend until smooth. Pour into a tall milkshake glass.

EGGNOG SHAKE

Servings: 1

A treat at holiday season.

1 shot espresso
2 oz. Swedish rum syrup
1 cup commercial eggnog
1 scoop eggnog or vanilla ice cream

In a blender, process espresso, syrup, eggnog and ice cream. Blend until smooth. Pour into a tall milkshake glass.

BANANA FUDGE SHAKE

Servings: 1

Use a frozen banana to give texture and flavor to this shake.

> 1 shot espresso
> 1 frozen banana, peeled and chunked
> 1 oz. banana syrup
> 1 oz. chocolate syrup
> ½ oz. vanilla syrup
> 1 cup milk
> 1 scoop chocolate ice cream

In a blender, process espresso, banana, syrup, milk and ice cream. Blend until smooth. Pour into a tall milkshake glass.

FROSTY THE SNOWMAN

Servings: 1

We're sure this one would win Frosty's approval. If your shakes are too thick, simply add more milk.

1 shot espresso
2 oz. peppermint syrup
1 cup milk
1 scoop peppermint ice cream

In a blender, process espresso, syrup, milk and ice cream. Blend until smooth. Pour into a tall milkshake glass.

BLACK CHERRY SHAKE

Servings: 1

Use vanilla, chocolate or cherry ice cream.

1 shot espresso
2 oz. cherry syrup
1 oz. chocolate syrup
1 cup milk
1 scoop vanilla ice cream

In a blender, process espresso, syrups, milk and ice cream. Blend until smooth. Pour into a tall milkshake glass.

NEAPOLITAN SHAKE

Servings: 1

You can also use a food processor with the steel knife to make these shakes.

> 1 shot espresso
> 1 oz. chocolate syrup
> 1 oz. strawberry syrup
> 1 oz. vanilla syrup
> 1 cup milk
> 1 scoop vanilla ice cream

In a blender, process espresso, syrups, milk and ice cream. Blend until smooth.

COFFEE KONA

Servings: 1

Slip on your head phones, put in your favorite CD and sip this delicious drink. Bliss.

1 cup espresso, chilled
1 oz. Tia Maria
2 oz. brandy
1 tbs. brown sugar
1 small scoop vanilla ice cream

Stir together espresso, Tia Maria, brandy and sugar until sugar dissolves. Top with ice cream. This is also good served hot and topped with whipped cream.

COFFEE COLA FLOAT

Servings: 1

This is one of those ideas that sound strange but taste great.

12 oz. cola
1 scoop coffee ice cream

In a 16-ounce soda fountain glass, combine cola and ice cream. Add a straw and enjoy.

BANANA COW

Servings: 1

Full of flavor!

1 shot espresso
1 oz. banana syrup
1 oz. chocolate syrup
½ oz. vanilla syrup
6 oz. soda
1 scoop vanilla or chocolate ice cream

In a tall milkshake glass, combine espresso and syrups. Stir well. Fill with soda and add ice cream.

BANANA SPLIT SODA

All the flavors of this ice cream treat in a glass. Garnish with whipped cream and a cherry!

1 oz. banana syrup
1 oz. chocolate syrup
1 oz. pineapple syrup
6 oz. soda
1 scoop banana ice cream

In a tall milkshake glass, combine espresso and syrups. Stir well. Fill with soda and add ice cream.

ICE CREAM ESPRESSO COOLER

Servings: 1

A popular license plate frame in Seattle states: **Powered by Espresso**.

1 cup cold milk
1 shot espresso
1 oz. French vanilla syrup
1 scoop vanilla ice cream
whipped cream
shaved chocolate for garnish

In a tall milkshake glass combine milk, espresso and syrup. Top with ice cream. Add whipped cream and garnish with shaved chocolate.

CHERRIES JUBILEE

Servings: 1

Dessert in a soda.

1 shot espresso
2 oz. bing cherry syrup
½ oz. rum syrup
6 oz. soda
1 scoop cherry or vanilla ice cream

In a tall milkshake glass, combine espresso and syrups. Stir well. Fill with soda and add ice cream.

CHOCOLATE CHIP MINT SODA

Servings: 1

This one will wake up your taste buds!

1 shot espresso
2 oz. chocolate mint syrup
1 oz. chocolate topping
6 oz. soda
1 scoop chocolate chip mint ice cream

In a tall milkshake glass, combine espresso and syrups. Stir well. Fill with soda and add ice cream.

INDEX

SERVE CREATIVE, EASY, NUTRITIOUS MEALS WITH nitty gritty® cookbooks

Fresh Vegetables
Cooking With Fresh Herbs
The Dehydrator Cookbook
Recipes for the Pressure Cooker
Beer and Good Food
Unbeatable Chicken Recipes
Gourmet Gifts
From Freezer, 'Fridge and Pantry
Edible Pockets for Every Meal
Cooking with Chile Peppers
Oven and Rotisserie Roasting
Risottos, Paellas and Other Rice
    Specialties
Muffins, Nut Breads and More
Healthy Snacks for Kids
100 Dynamite Desserts
Recipes for Yogurt Cheese
Sautés
Cooking in Porcelain
Appetizers
Casseroles
The Toaster Oven Cookbook
Skewer Cooking on the Grill
Creative Mexican Cooking
Marinades
The Wok

No Salt, No Sugar, No Fat Cookbook
Quick and Easy Pasta Recipes
Cooking in Clay
Deep Fried Indulgences
Cooking with Parchment Paper
The Garlic Cookbook
From Your Ice Cream Maker
Cappuccino/Espresso: The Book of
    Beverages
The Best Pizza is Made at Home
The Best Bagels are Made at Home
Convection Oven Cookery
The Steamer Cookbook
The Pasta Machine Cookbook
The Versatile Rice Cooker
The Bread Machine Cookbook
The Bread Machine Cookbook II
The Bread Machine Cookbook III
The Bread Machine Cookbook IV:
    Whole Grains and Natural Sugars

For a free catalog, write or call:
Bristol Publishing Enterprises, Inc.
P.O. Box 1737
San Leandro, CA 94577
(800) 346-4889
in California (510) 895-4461

The Bread Machine Cookbook V:
    Favorite Recipes from 100 Kitchens
The Bread Machine Cookbook VI:
    Hand-Shaped Breads form the
    Dough Cycle
Worldwide Sourdoughs from Your
    Bread Machine
Entrées From Your Bread Machine
The New Blender Book
The Sandwich Maker Cookbook
Waffles
The Coffee Book
The Juicer Books I and II
Bread Baking
The 9 x 13 Pan Cookbook
Recipes for the Loaf Pan
Low Fat American Favorites
Healthy Cooking on the Run
Favorite Seafood Recipes
New International Fondue
    Cookbook
Favorite Cookie Recipes
Cooking for 1 or 2
The Well Dressed Potato
Extra-Special Crockery Pot Recipes
Slow Cooking